Tyrus

Title: "Journey Through Time: The Enigmatic Life of Just Tyrus"

This enigmatic figure, Just Tyrus, seemed to possess an innate ability to navigate the turbulent currents of his era with an air of confidence and wisdom that defied explanation. His origins, veiled in obscurity, only added to the intrigue surrounding his persona. Legends and folklore intertwine with fragments of historical accounts, creating a tapestry of myths and truths that continues to captivate the imagination of those who seek to unravel the enigma of Just Tyrus.

Born in a realm unlike our own, Just Tyrus emerged into a world defined by epochs that shifted like tides, sweeping civilizations and empires across the stage of history. From the fragmented accounts that have survived, it becomes apparent that his life was intertwined with pivotal moments of upheaval and transformation. Whispers of his presence can be traced through ancient manuscripts, inscriptions on weathered stones, and the fading echoes of oral traditions passed down through generations.

Tales of his encounters with the great minds of his time evoke images of profound conversations that shaped the course of ideas and ideologies. Whether engaging in philosophical debates amidst the ruins of forgotten cities or seeking solace in the company of reclusive sages, Just Tyrus seemed drawn to the pursuit of knowledge and the exploration of the mysteries that lay beyond the veil of reality.

Yet, for all his intellectual pursuits, there were whispers of a deeper, more mystical aspect to his character. Legends speak of his involvement in arcane rituals and esoteric practices that blurred the boundaries between the material and the metaphysical. Some accounts even claim that he possessed a connection to forces beyond mortal understanding, a notion that fuels speculation about the true nature of his being.

As the epochs ebbed and flowed, Just Tyrus appeared to traverse lands both known and uncharted, leaving traces of his passage in the form of cryptic symbols and enigmatic artifacts. His legacy, though often obscured by the mists of time, continues to influence the currents of thought and creativity that shape our world today. Artists, scholars, and dreamers draw inspiration from the fragments of his story, weaving them into their own narratives as they strive to capture the essence of a man who defied the limitations of his era.

In the tapestry of history, Just Tyrus remains a figure whose true significance eludes easy classification. Was he a philosopher, a mystic, a time traveler, or something altogether beyond our comprehension? The truth, perhaps, resides in the interplay of fact and fantasy, where the boundaries between reality and imagination blur, inviting us to explore the depths of human potential and the mysteries that lie just beyond our grasp.

Chapter 1: Origins of Mystery

The journey of Just Tyrus began in the heart of a bygone era, where dusty tomes and ancient scrolls held the secrets of civilizations past. Details of his early life are scarce, but the threads of his existence can be traced to the bustling markets and scholarly enclaves of a time long before our own.

In the sprawling city of Arcanum, nestled between rolling hills and fertile valleys, Just Tyrus is believed to have taken his first breath. Arcanum was a center of knowledge and trade, where merchants haggled over exotic goods and scholars delved into the mysteries of the cosmos. Born to parents shrouded in anonymity, Just Tyrus's upbringing was marked by a sense of wanderlust and an insatiable curiosity that set him apart even from a young age.

Legend has it that he would often disappear for days, venturing into the city's labyrinthine alleys and hidden courtyards. He seemed drawn to the many libraries and schools that dotted the cityscape, devouring scrolls and manuscripts on subjects ranging from philosophy and history to alchemy and the arcane arts. Some accounts suggest that he possessed an uncanny ability to decipher ancient languages, unlocking the wisdom contained within texts that had long confounded scholars.

As he grew older, Just Tyrus's reputation as a prodigious intellect and an unquenchable seeker of truths spread throughout Arcanum. He became a fixture in the city's intellectual circles, engaging in debates that left seasoned philosophers pondering the depths of his insights. Yet, even as he delved into the intricacies of metaphysics and cosmology, there was an air of detachment about him, as if he were privy to a perspective that extended beyond the realm of mortal understanding.

It was during this time that rumors began to circulate about his encounters with mysterious figures who were said to possess knowledge beyond the boundaries of ordinary human experience. Some whispered that he conversed with spectral entities under moonlit skies, while others claimed he communed with ancient spirits in the depths of forgotten ruins. These accounts, though often dismissed as mere folklore, contributed to the aura of mystique that surrounded him.

But it was a chance discovery within the crumbling catacombs beneath Arcanum that set Just Tyrus on a path that would forever alter the course of his life. Amongst the forgotten chambers and dimly lit passages, he stumbled upon an intricately carved amulet, pulsating with an otherworldly energy. The amulet seemed to resonate with his very essence, awakening dormant faculties within him and granting him glimpses of realms beyond the physical.

From that moment, Just Tyrus's journey took a turn into the realm of the uncanny and the uncharted. His pursuit of knowledge evolved into an exploration of the esoteric and the enigmatic, as he sought to unlock the secrets that lay hidden beneath the surface of reality. His encounters with the arcane grew more frequent, and his reputation as a bridge between worlds cemented his place as a figure of fascination and awe.

As whispers of his exploits spread far beyond the boundaries of Arcanum, a network of seekers, scholars, and mystics began to emerge, drawn by the allure of Just Tyrus's insights. The enigma of his origins only deepened the intrigue surrounding him, as questions multiplied: Was he a prodigy of nature, a chosen vessel, or a being from a distant age?

In the next chapter of his journey, the tapestry of Just Tyrus's life would weave through uncharted territories and encounters that defied the boundaries of time and space. As he ventured into the unknown, his legacy would become interwoven with the very fabric of reality itself.

Chapter 2: A Scholar of Eras

Tyrus emerged as a beacon of knowledge, his insatiable curiosity driving him to explore a myriad of subjects that spanned the breadth of human understanding. From the mystical arts of alchemy to the intricacies of celestial navigation, he traversed through the corridors of knowledge, leaving behind a trail of manuscripts and treatises that would perplex and inspire generations to come.

Having honed his intellectual prowess in the scholarly enclaves of Arcanum, Just Tyrus embarked on a journey that would take him across distant lands and eras. His insatiable thirst for knowledge led him to venture into realms both familiar and alien, as he sought to uncover the underlying truths that connected disparate fields of study.

Alchemy, a discipline that straddled the line between science and spirituality, held a particular fascination for Tyrus. He delved into the esoteric teachings of transmutation, seeking to unveil the hidden forces that bound matter and spirit. His experiments with alchemical processes yielded both successes and failures, and his cryptic writings on the subject would become the subject of heated debates among alchemists for generations to come.

But his interests did not stop at the threshold of the material world. Astronomy and celestial navigation beckoned to him, and he spent nights beneath star-strewn skies, charting the movements of constellations and planets. It was said that he possessed a celestial map that extended beyond the scope of ordinary understanding, allowing him to navigate the cosmos with an uncanny precision. Whispers arose that he had gazed upon distant stars that were invisible to the naked eye, and that he had conversed with celestial beings who whispered cosmic secrets into his ear.

In the courts of emperors and the chambers of scholars, Just Tyrus held court as a sage whose insights transcended the boundaries of time. He expounded upon the nature of reality, weaving intricate theories that blended the metaphysical with the scientific. His teachings often provoked awe and skepticism in equal measure, challenging the accepted norms of his era and inviting others to expand their horizons of thought.

Yet, even as his reputation as a scholar of eras grew, so too did the rumors surrounding his origins and abilities. Some claimed that he possessed the ability to glimpse into the future or to traverse the currents of time itself. Whether these notions were borne of truth or embellishment, they further enshrouded his persona in an aura of mystery and fascination.

As Tyrus traversed the landscapes of ancient civilizations, he left behind a trail of manuscripts, treatises, and cryptic symbols. His writings often defied conventional categorization, blending philosophy, mysticism, and scientific observation into a tapestry of ideas that transcended the limitations of language. Scholars and seekers who followed in his wake would find themselves deciphering his works for centuries, attempting to unlock the wisdom he had amassed over his enigmatic existence.

His legacy was one of both inspiration and bewilderment, inviting future generations to peer into the enigma of his life and the boundless frontiers of knowledge he had explored. The echoes of his ideas would reverberate through the corridors of time, leaving an indelible mark on the collective consciousness of humanity. Just Tyrus, the scholar of eras, would continue to guide the curious and the intrepid toward the horizon of discovery, where the mysteries of existence beckoned like distant stars in the night sky.

Chapter 3: The Time Traveler's Odyssey

It was whispered that Just Tyrus possessed a power that transcended the boundaries of time itself. Rumors abound of his clandestine journeys, tales that recount his encounters with civilizations long forgotten and the luminaries who shaped the world's course. These time-traveling escapades, if true, present a tapestry of adventure and intrigue that defy the limits of human comprehension.

As the enigma of Just Tyrus's life continued to deepen, whispers grew louder regarding his alleged ability to traverse the currents of time. Stories emerged from the annals of history, tales told in hushed tones by those who claimed to have witnessed his time-traveling escapades firsthand. It was said that he possessed a device, an artifact of unfathomable origin, that granted him the power to breach the barriers between eras.

In these tales, Just Tyrus was depicted as a spectral figure, materializing amidst civilizations long lost to the sands of time. From the majestic courts of ancient Egypt to the bustling streets of medieval Byzantium, he moved like a shadow, an observer who bore witness to the rise and fall of empires. His presence in these historical epochs was often linked to pivotal moments and the fates of great minds.

In ancient Alexandria, it was rumored that he had shared philosophical discourse with the luminaries of the Library of Alexandria, engaging in debates that shaped the course of thought for generations to come. In the company of philosophers and scholars, he pondered the nature of existence and the boundaries of human understanding.

In the Renaissance halls of Florence, he was said to have exchanged ideas with the likes of Leonardo da Vinci and Galileo Galilei, sharing insights that spurred innovation and intellectual progress. Some accounts even suggest that he provided guidance to artists, scientists, and inventors, influencing their works in ways that shaped the trajectory of human history.

And so, the whispers persisted, recounting his appearances in eras both distant and recent. Some claimed to have seen him walking the battlefields of wars long past, while others spoke of his presence at pivotal moments in the quest for civil rights and social justice. These stories wove a tapestry of adventure and intrigue, presenting Just Tyrus as a timeless traveler who existed outside the confines of a linear existence.

Yet, the truth behind these tales remains shrouded in uncertainty. Were these accounts embellished legends, the product of an overactive imagination? Or did Just Tyrus truly possess the ability to navigate the currents of time, leaving a trail of influence across the epochs? Regardless of the veracity of the stories, the allure of his alleged time-traveling odyssey continues to captivate those who seek to understand the mysteries of his life.

In the intricate weave of history, Just Tyrus emerges as a figure who defies easy classification, blurring the lines between reality and myth. Whether a scholar of eras, a traveler of time, or something even more extraordinary, his legacy persists as a beacon that guides humanity's quest for knowledge, understanding, and the exploration of the enigmatic realms that lie beyond the veil of the known.

Chapter 4: Legacy of Influence

Though his presence in the historical record remains elusive, the ripples of Just Tyrus's influence are felt across epochs. His treatises on knowledge preservation and his revolutionary ideas on the interconnectedness of time and space have inspired thinkers, philosophers, and scientists throughout the ages. The very fabric of his ideas has woven itself into the fabric of progress.

While the details of Just Tyrus's life might forever remain shrouded in mystery, his impact on human thought and exploration is undeniable. His writings, those cryptic and profound treatises that spanned the gamut of human understanding, continue to be studied and interpreted by scholars of every generation. His ideas on knowledge preservation, for instance, laid the groundwork for libraries, archives, and institutions dedicated to safeguarding the wisdom of civilizations from the ravages of time.

The concept of interconnectedness that he expounded upon has resonated deeply with philosophers and scientists alike. Long before the advent of modern theories in physics, Tyrus mused about the fluid relationship between time, space, and the human experience. His musings on the delicate balance between destiny and free will have inspired debates that span centuries, illuminating the eternal struggle to understand the intricate tapestry of existence.

In the age of enlightenment, Tyrus's ideas experienced a resurgence, with philosophers drawing parallels between his concepts and the emerging scientific paradigms. The notion of a unified theory of existence, where all knowledge is interconnected, echoes in the works of thinkers like Isaac Newton and Immanuel Kant. Just Tyrus's influence can be seen in the very foundations of the Scientific Revolution, where the quest for knowledge reached new heights.

Even as technology progressed and humanity ventured beyond the confines of Earth, the echoes of Just Tyrus's legacy reverberated through space exploration. Astronomers pondered his writings on celestial navigation, finding inspiration in his explorations of the cosmos. The dream of charting the stars and understanding the universe's intricacies became a reality, and humanity's journey into the unknown was imbued with the spirit of curiosity and wonder that Tyrus personified.

In the modern era, his ideas continue to inspire those who seek to bridge the gaps between disciplines and explore the boundaries of human potential. Theories in quantum physics hint at the blurred lines between matter and energy that he mused upon, while the search for deeper understanding of time itself resonates with his musings on the interconnected nature of past, present, and future.

In the tapestry of history, Just Tyrus remains an enigmatic figure whose legacy transcends time. Whether a scholar, a time traveler, or a philosopher of eras, his presence endures through the currents of human thought. The ripples of his influence continue to shape the course of progress, guiding humanity toward a greater understanding of the mysteries that lie beyond the horizon of knowledge. As the epochs unfold, the enigma of Just Tyrus remains, an eternal source of inspiration for those who dare to explore the uncharted realms of existence.

Chapter 5: The Unveiling of Just Tyrus

The modern world, with its technological prowess, continues to unlock fragments of the past, casting light on figures like Just Tyrus. Historians, scientists, and enthusiasts, driven by an insatiable hunger for the truth, piece together fragments of his existence from ancient texts, cryptic symbols, and whispered folklore.

As humanity's quest for knowledge reached new heights in the digital age, so too did the efforts to unveil the enigma of Just Tyrus. Advanced imaging technology and the power of computational analysis breathed life into faded manuscripts and inscriptions, revealing hidden details and shedding light on his life and times. Collaborative efforts among scholars from diverse fields sought to decode the intricate patterns of his writings, uncovering layers of meaning that had long been concealed.

Archaeological expeditions embarked on journeys to remote locales, excavating forgotten ruins and unearthing artifacts that held clues to the past. In the process, they unearthed references to Just Tyrus—mentions in obscure scrolls, depictions in ancient murals—that painted a more vivid picture of his presence in history. These findings, while still incomplete, added brushstrokes to the portrait of a figure whose influence spanned across the ages.

Technology also allowed for a global exchange of information and ideas. Enthusiasts and amateur historians collaborated with experts, sharing discoveries and theories that collectively wove a narrative of Just Tyrus's life. Virtual symposiums and online forums became hubs of discussion, where individuals from different corners of the world could collectively contribute to the unraveling of his story.

As the modern world grappled with the tantalizing possibility of time travel and the intricacies of parallel dimensions, Just Tyrus's alleged time-traveling escapades took on new resonance. Theoretical physicists and cosmologists explored the boundaries of reality, delving into the mysteries of quantum mechanics and the nature of spacetime. His ideas, once considered the musings of a bygone era, found new relevance in the context of contemporary scientific discourse.

Even as the shroud of mystery was lifted, questions lingered. Was Just Tyrus a product of an advanced civilization, one that transcended the limitations of time? Or was he a unique individual who had stumbled upon cosmic truths that granted him unparalleled insights? The truth, it seemed, was a tapestry woven from fragments of history, legend, and speculation.

The unveiling of Just Tyrus did not diminish his enigma; instead, it deepened the fascination that had surrounded him for centuries. The more that was revealed, the more questions arose. In a world where technology and human curiosity intersect, the journey to understand Just Tyrus continues, a testament to the unyielding spirit of exploration that drives humanity forward.

In the modern era, as the threads of knowledge continue to intertwine, Just Tyrus stands as a figure whose life and legacy resonate across time. His story is a reminder that even in the face of the unknown, the pursuit of understanding is a journey that transcends eras, unifying past, present, and the boundless future.

Conclusion:

Just Tyrus, a name whispered through the corridors of history, stands as a testament to the enduring power of curiosity and the human quest for understanding. His life, draped in the enigmatic veil of time, serves as a reminder that even in the depths of uncertainty, the pursuit of knowledge transcends the ages, uniting generations in an eternal quest for truth. As we continue to unlock the secrets of his life, may Just Tyrus inspire us to reach beyond the confines of our own era and explore the boundless realms of possibility that await. In a world where mysteries abound and the tapestry of history weaves its intricate patterns, may we carry his legacy as a torch, illuminating the uncharted territories of thought, discovery, and imagination that lie ahead. Just Tyrus, the enigma, the scholar, the time traveler—his name lives on as an echo in the corridors of time, guiding us toward the unending pursuit of enlightenment.

George Murdoch, born on February 21, 1973, is a multifaceted American personality known by his ring/stage name Tyrus. He has made his mark as a professional wrestler, cable news commentator, and actor. In the world of wrestling, he is associated with the National Wrestling Alliance (NWA), where he holds the title of NWA Worlds Heavyweight Champion in his first reign. As a cable news figure, he is a familiar face on Fox News and its streaming platform Fox Nation, frequently seen as a co-host and panelist on the late-night talk show "Gutfeld!" while also contributing and filling in as a host on other programs.

Tyrus began his wrestling journey by undergoing training in WWE's developmental territories, including Deep South Wrestling (DSW) and Florida Championship Wrestling (FCW). He made his first appearance as Brodus Clay during the fourth season of NXT, a WWE television show that paired rookies with established mentors. Initially, he joined the main roster as the bodyguard of Alberto Del Rio. In 2012, his wrestling persona underwent a transformation, and he adopted the gimmick of "The Funkasaurus," a funk dancer accompanied by his backup dancers, known as the Funkadactyls. He remained a part of WWE until his departure in 2014.

Following his time in WWE, Murdoch shifted to Total Nonstop Action Wrestling (TNA), now known as Impact Wrestling, where he wrestled under the name Tyrus from 2014 to 2017. In 2021, he made his way to the NWA, where he achieved success by capturing the NWA World Television Championship and subsequently the promotion's premier title, the Worlds Heavyweight Championship.

In 2022, Murdoch added the accomplishment of being a New York Times bestselling author to his repertoire with his autobiography "Just Tyrus: A Memoir." This publication sheds light on his life, experiences, and journey, providing readers with insights into the man behind the various roles he's played throughout his career.

George Murdoch, also known as Tyrus, embodies the diversity of talent and skills that can thrive across different domains, from the wrestling ring to the realm of media and entertainment. His dynamic presence and achievements continue to captivate audiences, making him a noteworthy figure in both wrestling and the public eye.

Early life

George Murdoch's early life was marked by a series of challenges and experiences that would shape his future endeavors. Murdoch, who later gained fame as Tyrus, was born biracial, with a black father and a white mother. He was born when his father was 19 years old and his mother was 15, a situation that added to the complexity of his upbringing.

In 2018, Murdoch revealed a traumatic incident from his childhood in which his abusive father caused damage to his eye by physically hitting him. This incident led to his mother leaving his father. Murdoch's mother returned to her parents' home, but Murdoch and his brother did not find acceptance there due to their mixed racial heritage. Instead, Murdoch and his brother lived with a foster family for a significant period. During this time, Murdoch became fixated on the idea of changing his skin color, believing that it might facilitate reuniting with his family.

While he eventually reunited with his mother and brother, Murdoch's journey remained challenging. His early life experiences prompted him to leave home at the young age of 15 in search of a path that he could call his own.

Throughout his educational journey, Murdoch's determination and resilience were evident. He attended Quartz Hill High School in Los Angeles County, California, and then pursued higher education at Antelope Valley College in Lancaster. By 1995, he had enrolled at the University of Nebraska at Kearney, where he focused on studying to become a teacher. During his time there, he also played college football for the Lopers, showcasing his athleticism and dedication to his pursuits.

However, his football aspirations were halted by a medical setback. A surgery to remove a ruptured appendix led to nerve damage in his leg, resulting in a permanent limp that marked the end of his football career.

In addition to his endeavors in education and sports, Murdoch's life took an interesting turn when he worked as a bodyguard for the renowned rapper Snoop Dogg. This experience, while not extensively detailed, adds another layer to the diverse range of roles that Murdoch would go on to assume in his life and career.

The challenges and experiences of George Murdoch's early life, from his complex family dynamics to his determination in education and athletics, laid the foundation for the multifaceted journey that would lead him to his roles as Tyrus the professional wrestler, media personality, and more. His ability to overcome adversity and evolve from his past experiences serves as a testament to his resilience and his drive to succeed in the face of obstacles.

Professional wrestling career
World Wrestling Entertainment / WWE

G-Rilla at an FCW event in 2007
Developmental territories (2006–2008)

During the years 2006 to 2008, George Murdoch embarked on his journey within the World Wrestling Entertainment (WWE) organization, beginning with his assignment to the developmental territory, Deep South Wrestling (DSW). This period marked his initial foray into the wrestling industry and the development of his wrestling persona under various ring names and gimmicks.

Deep South Wrestling (DSW) Development (2006-2008):

After signing a contract with WWE, Murdoch was assigned to Deep South Wrestling (DSW), a developmental territory where aspiring wrestlers hone their skills before moving to the main WWE roster. He made his debut in September 2006 under the ring name "G-Rilla" and embraced the persona of a street thug. His first match was a victory against Big Bully Douglas in a dark match on September 7, 2006.

In the following months, G-Rilla became the enforcer for a tag team called Urban Assault, consisting of Eric Pérez and Sonny Siaki. However, conflicts arose, including a feud with The Bag Lady, which caused challenges for Urban Assault's championship pursuits. Despite capturing the DSW Tag Team Championship from The Major Brothers (Brian and Brett), tensions within the group led to G-Rilla's removal from Urban Assault after altercations with Bag Lady and her ally, Freakin' Deacon.

In early 2007, G-Rilla turned against Urban Assault, attacking its members during matches. He then formed an unlikely tag team partnership with former adversary Freakin' Deacon. The duo successfully defeated various opponents, including members of Urban Assault, and even managed to defeat the reigning DSW Tag Team Champions, Team Elite.

However, the team's momentum was short-lived. A storyline involving Freakin' Deacon's brutal assault and subsequent mental breakdown marked the dissolution of their partnership. In June 2007, Murdoch transitioned to Florida Championship Wrestling (FCW), another WWE developmental territory, and made his debut as G-Rilla.

Florida Championship Wrestling (FCW) and WWE Release (2007-2008):

Murdoch's time in FCW continued to showcase his evolution as a wrestler. He engaged in rivalries and alliances with other emerging talents and established wrestlers. During his time in FCW, he feuded with the likes of Harry Smith and Teddy Hart, participating in a series of matches and storylines.

Unfortunately, Murdoch's journey with WWE came to an end in February 2008 when he was released from his contract. This marked a hiatus from the wrestling scene that would last for the next two years.

While his initial stint in WWE developmental territories was marked by various ring names, partnerships, and storylines, it laid the groundwork for his eventual transformation into Tyrus, a persona that would be recognized in the larger wrestling world and beyond. His experiences during this developmental phase were pivotal in shaping his skills, character, and future in the wrestling industry.

NXT and Alliance with Alberto Del Rio (2010–2011):

After a hiatus of two years, George Murdoch made his return to WWE in January 2010. He re-signed with the company and was once again assigned to Florida Championship Wrestling (FCW) to further develop his skills. During this period, Murdoch underwent several changes in his wrestling identity as he navigated his path through the developmental system.

Formation of The Colossal Connection (2010):

Under the name G-Rilla, Murdoch formed an alliance with The Uso Brothers, Tamina, and Donny Marlow in FCW in March 2010. This alliance showcased his ability to work in a team dynamic and led to various tag team matches and storylines. In May 2010, Murdoch adopted a new ring name, Brodus Clay, which played off the real name of rapper Snoop Dogg (Calvin Cordozar Broadus). This marked the start of a new chapter in his wrestling journey.

NXT Debut and Alberto Del Rio's Pro (2010–2011):

Brodus Clay's journey into the NXT reality show began during the fourth season. He was paired with professional wrestlers Ted DiBiase and Maryse as his mentors. He made his in-ring debut on NXT in December 2010, teaming with DiBiase to defeat Byron Saxton and Chris Masters.

Clay's journey within NXT continued as he won a four-way elimination match, earning the right to choose a new mentor. He selected the established wrestler Alberto Del Rio as his new mentor, leading to a series of developments and conflicts. Clay's alliance with Del Rio included an attack on DiBiase and a subsequent singles match victory over him. Del Rio's responsibilities as Clay's mentor were temporarily passed on to his manager Ricardo Rodriguez.

Despite his efforts in NXT, Clay finished in second place during the season finale, ultimately losing to Johnny Curtis. However, his appearance on NXT paved the way for his transition to the main WWE roster.

Alliance with Alberto Del Rio and Matches (2011):

After his NXT run, Brodus Clay debuted on the main roster of WWE. On the March 7, 2011 episode of Raw, he appeared as Alberto Del Rio's new bodyguard, replacing Del Rio in a match against Christian. This marked the beginning of their alliance, with Clay accompanying Del Rio to the ring for various matches and events.

Their partnership involved feuds with wrestlers like Edge and Christian, leading to singles matches and tag team contests. Clay's role was to support Del Rio in his rivalries, including accompanying him to WrestleMania XXVII for a match against Edge.

Despite Del Rio's draft to Raw, Clay remained on SmackDown and continued his alliance with Del Rio. However, their partnership began to unravel, with Clay's final appearance alongside Del Rio occurring at Extreme Rules in May 2011.

After a brief hiatus due to filming commitments, Clay returned to WWE programming on the August 4, 2011 episode of Superstars, where he faced and defeated various lower-card wrestlers in squash matches.

This period showcased Brodus Clay's evolution from his developmental years in FCW to his role as a bodyguard and ally of Alberto Del Rio on the main WWE roster. The various twists and turns in his journey laid the foundation for his subsequent transformations and contributions in the world of professional wrestling.

The Funkasaurus Era (2012–2014):

During this period, George Murdoch portrayed the character Brodus Clay, who underwent a dramatic transformation into "The Funkasaurus." This phase marked a notable shift in his wrestling persona, showcasing a colorful and energetic gimmick that emphasized dancing, charisma, and audience engagement.

Introduction of The Funkasaurus (2012):

After months of promotional vignettes, Brodus Clay made his television return to WWE programming on the January 9, 2012 episode of Raw. This marked the debut of his new persona, "The Funkasaurus," a fun-loving and charismatic character known for his dance moves and lively antics. Accompanied by The Funkadactyls (Naomi and Cameron), Clay was announced as hailing from "Planet Funk" and adopted the entrance theme "Somebody Call My Momma," originally associated with wrestler Ernest "The Cat" Miller.

Character Development and Feuds (2012–2013):

Clay's Funkasaurus character quickly gained attention and popularity among fans. He incorporated dance routines and gyrations into his matches, often defeating opponents in squash matches on Raw and SmackDown. Clay's wrestling style and personality set him apart from his peers, creating an entertaining spectacle for the audience.

His memorable appearance at WrestleMania XXVIII, where he danced with Momma Clay (Ernest Miller), and his ongoing streak of squash match victories contributed to his appeal. He was involved in feuds with wrestlers like Dolph Ziggler and Jack Swagger, leading to tag team victories alongside Santino Marella.

Tag Team with Tensai as "Tons of Funk" (2013):

In 2013, Clay's character underwent further development as he formed a tag team with Tensai (formerly known as Albert and A-Train). Together, they embraced the name "Tons of Funk" and gained popularity for their entertaining entrances, dance routines, and camaraderie. They secured victories over established tag teams like Primo & Epico, Heath Slater and Jinder Mahal of 3MB, and Team Rhodes Scholars (Cody Rhodes and Damien Sandow).

Heel Turn and Later Departure (2013–2014):

However, Clay's character trajectory took a significant turn. In late 2013, he started displaying villainous tendencies, becoming jealous of the debuting Xavier Woods, who incorporated elements of Clay's character into his own entrance. This marked the beginning of a heel turn for Clay, as he began attacking Woods and R-Truth, showcasing a more aggressive and antagonistic side.

By mid-2014, Clay's character underwent further changes, and he found himself facing losses in matches against Woods, Truth, and others. On June 12, 2014, WWE announced that Clay had been released from his contract, marking the end of his time with the company.

The Funkasaurus era, while relatively short-lived, remains a memorable chapter in Brodus Clay's wrestling journey. His colorful character, dance-filled entrances, and interactions with fellow wrestlers added a unique and entertaining dimension to WWE programming during this period.

Total Nonstop Action Wrestling / Impact Wrestling (2014–2018):

In this phase of his career, George Murdoch, under the ring name Tyrus, entered the world of Total Nonstop Action Wrestling (TNA), which later became Impact Wrestling. His time in TNA/Impact Wrestling showcased various storylines, partnerships, and challenges that added depth to his wrestling journey.

Debut and Partnership with Ethan Carter III (2014–2015):

Tyrus made his debut for TNA on September 16, 2014, aligning himself with Ethan Carter III (EC3). He quickly became EC3's enforcer and ally, adding a physically imposing presence to EC3's character. His wrestling skills and power were put to the test as he participated in matches, often alongside EC3.

Tyrus's first wrestling match in TNA was against Shark Boy on the October 15, 2014 episode of Impact Wrestling, which he won. He and EC3 entered the TNA World Tag Team Championship number one contenders tournament, showcasing their partnership in the tag team division.

Singles Matches and Character Evolution (2015–2017):

Tyrus continued to engage in singles matches and storylines, participating in matches against Mr. Anderson and others. His role as EC3's enforcer remained a defining aspect of his character. At Slammiversary, Tyrus and EC3 secured a victory against Lashley and Mr. Anderson in the co-main event.

Tyrus's character underwent further development in 2016 when he returned as a "fixer" for hire, aligning himself with wrestlers like Grado and Mahabali Shera. This new persona showcased his versatility and ability to adapt to different roles within the wrestling world. His partnership with Eli Drake marked another notable phase of his Impact Wrestling tenure, leading to tag team matches and challenges against other teams.

Release and Return (2017–2018):

Tyrus's journey within Impact Wrestling experienced a shift in 2017 when he was granted his release from his contract in August. His decision to leave was reportedly influenced by concerns about the direction of the promotion under the leadership of Jeff Jarrett.

Despite his departure, Tyrus made a return to Impact Wrestling in early 2018, engaging in a storyline that saw him defeat his former ally Ethan Carter III. However, his return was short-lived, and he confirmed his release and departure from the company in April 2018. Murdoch cited creative and booking decisions that he felt would negatively impact his character's reputation as a reason for his departure.

Tyrus's time in TNA/Impact Wrestling showcased his ability to adapt to various character roles, his in-ring skills, and his contributions to storylines alongside different wrestlers. His journey within the promotion added another layer of experience to his wrestling career.

Independent Circuit (2018):

After his departure from Impact Wrestling, George Murdoch, using his ring name Tyrus, ventured into the independent wrestling circuit to continue his wrestling journey. This phase allowed him to explore new opportunities and showcase his skills in various promotions outside of the larger wrestling organizations.

House of Hardcore Debut (2018):

Tyrus made his debut in Tommy Dreamer's promotion, House of Hardcore, at House of Hardcore 52 on December 8, 2018. In this event, he teamed up with Robert Strauss (also known as Robbie E in Impact Wrestling) to face the team of David Arquette and RJ City. While Tyrus and Strauss formed a tag team, they were unsuccessful in their match against Arquette and City.

Participating in independent promotions like House of Hardcore allowed Tyrus to interact with different talents, engage in unique storylines, and entertain audiences beyond the confines of mainstream wrestling organizations.

This phase of his career demonstrated his willingness to explore various wrestling platforms and continue his connection with wrestling fans in different settings.

National Wrestling Alliance (2021–present)
NWA World Television Champion (2021–2022)

NWA World Television Champion (2021-2022):

In this phase of his career, Tyrus found success in the National Wrestling Alliance (NWA), capturing both the NWA World Television Championship and the NWA Worlds Heavyweight Championship, marking significant milestones in his wrestling journey.

NWA World Television Championship Reign (2021-2022):

Tyrus made his NWA debut on March 11, 2021, at Back For The Attack, where he defeated Kratos. He quickly climbed the ranks in the NWA, earning a shot at the NWA World Television Championship. On August 6, 2021, Tyrus achieved a major accomplishment by defeating The Pope (Elijah Burke) to win the NWA World Television Championship.

During his reign as champion, Tyrus successfully defended the NWA World Television Championship against various contenders, showcasing his ability to hold his own against a range of opponents. He faced challenges from wrestlers like BLK Jeez, Jordan Clearwater, Cyon, Jaden Roller, Rodney Mack, Mims, and Odinson.

NWA Worlds Heavyweight Champion (2022-present):
Tyrus's journey continued as he set his sights on the ultimate prize in the NWA: the NWA Worlds Heavyweight Championship. He challenged Trevor Murdoch for the championship at the NWA 74th Anniversary Show on August 28, 2022, but was unsuccessful in capturing the title at that time.
However, Tyrus's opportunity for championship glory was not lost. On November 12, 2022, at NWA Hard Times 3, Tyrus managed to defeat Trevor Murdoch, pinning him to become the NWA Worlds Heavyweight Champion. This victory marked a significant milestone in Tyrus's career as he captured his first world championship.
Tyrus's title reign saw him successfully defend the NWA Worlds Heavyweight Championship in matches against notable opponents such as Matt Cardona and Chris Adonis. He even formed a tag team named "The Midnight Riders" with Adonis and competed in the Crockett Cup tournament.
His time in the NWA not only saw him achieve championship success but also solidified his status as a top competitor in the promotion, further adding to the diverse tapestry of his wrestling journey.

Television commentary career

Media and Television Career:

After his wrestling career, George Murdoch, known as Tyrus, transitioned into the world of media and television, becoming a prominent figure on Fox News Channel and Fox Nation. His charisma and presence from the wrestling world translated well into his role as a commentator and host on various programs.

Guest Commentator and Regular Contributor on Fox News:

In November 2016, Tyrus made his debut as a guest commentator on "The Greg Gutfeld Show," hosted by Greg Gutfeld on Fox News. His appearances were well-received, leading to Gutfeld inviting him back to the show twice a month. Tyrus appeared under his wrestling stage name, becoming a recognizable presence on the network.

His appearances extended beyond "The Greg Gutfeld Show." He made guest appearances on other Fox News programs, including "The Five." Tyrus's unique perspective and engaging presence made him a valuable contributor to the network's lineup.

Regular Panelist on "Gutfeld!":

Tyrus's association with Greg Gutfeld continued to evolve, and he became a regular panelist on "Gutfeld!," a late-night show hosted by Greg Gutfeld that relaunched in April 2021 at 11 p.m. This marked another step in his media career, as he provided commentary and insights on a variety of topics alongside other panelists.

Other Hosting Endeavors:

Tyrus's involvement extended beyond Fox News Channel to Fox Nation, the network's streaming service. From 2018 to 2019, he co-hosted the show "Un-PC" on Fox Nation, where he engaged in discussions and debates on current events and various subjects.

In June 2019, Tyrus premiered his own Fox Nation show called "Nuff Said." This new show provided him with a platform to express his opinions and insights on different topics, further showcasing his abilities as a host and commentator.

Political Stance and Personal Life:

Tyrus's media career and political opinions intersected, as he was known to be a supporter of former President Donald Trump. However, it was noted that he did not vote in the 2016 election, and it remains unclear whether he voted in subsequent elections.

Overall, George Murdoch's transition from wrestling to media allowed him to showcase his charisma, wit, and unique perspective in a new realm. His presence on Fox News and Fox Nation marked another chapter in his multi-faceted career journey.

Sexual Harassment Allegation and Lawsuit:

In 2019, a sexual harassment allegation emerged involving Tyrus (George Murdoch) and his co-host on the Fox News show "Un-PC," Britt McHenry. According to reports, McHenry accused Murdoch of sending her a series of lewd text messages, which prompted an investigation into the matter.

Accusation and Investigation:

Britt McHenry alleged that Tyrus sent her inappropriate and lewd text messages, which raised concerns of sexual harassment. Fox News, the network on which "Un-PC" aired, initiated an investigation into the allegations.

Legal Action:
Despite the network's investigation and resolution, on December 10, 2019, Britt McHenry filed a sexual harassment lawsuit against both Fox News and George Murdoch (Tyrus). The lawsuit likely sought to address the allegations and seek remedies for the alleged harassment.

Lawsuit Resolution and Departure:
In the course of the legal proceedings, Britt McHenry later claimed that she lost the phone containing text messages that she believed were crucial to her claims. However, in July 2021, McHenry voluntarily dismissed the lawsuit. Additionally, she left the Fox network, which suggests that her departure may have been part of a legal settlement between the parties involved.

The case shed light on issues of workplace behavior and highlighted the steps taken by Fox News to address such allegations. The details of the lawsuit's resolution and any related settlements were not explicitly provided in the information you've provided.

Filmography of George Murdoch (Tyrus):

George Murdoch, known as Tyrus, has a diverse filmography that includes appearances in films and television shows spanning different genres. Here is a list of some of his notable roles in both film and television:

Film:

2012 - No One Lives: Murdoch played the role of Ethan in this film.

2014 - Scooby-Doo! WrestleMania Mystery: Murdoch provided his voice for the character Brodus Clay in this animated film.

2017 - Enuattii: He portrayed the character Bateman in this film.

2017 - Supercon: Murdoch appeared as a Security Guard in this film.

2020 - Stand On It: He played the role of Sheriff Cletus T. Necessary.

2021 - Poker Run: Murdoch portrayed the character Cletus T. Necessary in this film.

Television:

2013 - Total Divas: He appeared as himself in three episodes of this reality television series.

2014 - Trashville: Murdoch played the role of Danye East in the episode "Meeting the Maker."

2016-present - Gutfeld!: He is a regular panelist on this show, contributing his insights and opinions.

2017 - GLOW: Murdoch appeared as Mighty Tom Jackson in two episodes of this television series.

2017 - Preacher: He portrayed the character Hell Guard in three episodes of this show.

2017 - Syn: Murdoch played the role of Dylan in 13 episodes of this series.

2017 - MacGyver: He appeared as Goliath in one episode.

2018 - Love: Murdoch portrayed the character Keith the Creamator in one episode.

2018 - The Purge: He played the role of Gate Guard in the episode "Release the Beast."

2019 - Nuff Said: Murdoch hosted this show, appearing as himself.

Made in United States
Troutdale, OR
01/22/2024

17074689R00030